I am Reggie...

Life from the eyes of an exceptionally different boy

Written By: T.L. Tucker

Illustrations By: Blueberry Illustrations

Copyright © 2013 by T. L. Tucker

Printed in USA
ISBN: 9780692546000
Published on 10/06/2015

About the Illustrator
Blueberry Illustrations is one of the finest illustration companies in the world. Specializing in children's book illustration, blueberry Illustrations has won many international awards, and has published upwards of 112 books with many more in the making. Every book we publish is special and designed to bring a smile to the faces of millions of children worldwide. To learn more, please visit us at
www.blueberryillustrations.com
or contact us at blueberryillustrations@gmail.com

Dedication

This book is dedicated to all of the children that were born exceptionally different. God loves you! You are unique and beautiful. You are amongst God's favored people and He created you with a great purpose in mind!

To all the parents that were blessed with exceptionally different children: God loves you and your children. He only gives special children to special parents, with special hearts. He knew that you were a parent warrior! He would only leave a task like this to a very few and elite group of people. You are favored too.

To Sabrina and Reginald: I love you and you inspire all good things in me.
You are my gifts from God

In the enchanted city of Glenardia lives a boy named Reginald David , but everybody calls him Reggie. He is a very loving and happy child, and created by God as a prince of royalty.

Reggie knew that he was a special boy. His parents were worried because they saw early on that he was very different from other children.

Reggie did not speak, but he always made his feelings very clear. He would make the most beautiful noises that nobody could understand. It was his secret way of talking to God.

Every time Reggie was out people would whisper and stare. Some people would even laugh and make fun of Reggie because he was different. It seemed that no matter what people would say, Reggie's smile would still shine brighter than the sun.

Reggie was happy to be different. It didn't make him sad that people treated him mean. He was happy to be who he was.

One day as Reggie happily played in the sandbox at the playground, all of the other children gathered around him. They were pointing, laughing, and calling him names.

Reggie looked up into the sky smiling, and made the loudest most beautiful noise that he had ever made before.

As all of the children laughed, suddenly there appeared a little old woman. She wore glasses and her hair was silvery grey and pulled back. As she came closer to the sandbox, all of the children were scared to silence. They knew deep down that what they were doing was wrong, and was afraid that they would be in big trouble.

All eyes were on this little old lady, whose very presence seemed to glow. Reggie slowly stood up and walked over to the bench where the little old lady rested. The other children followed. The little old lady looked at Reggie and touched his face lovingly.

"Hello," she said. "My name is Miss Angelica. I couldn't help but overhear you teasing Reggie. Why were you all being so mean to him?"

One little boy by the name of Joey yelled out, "Why doesn't he talk?"
Another little girl by the name of Sarah said, "He never wants to play with us, and he makes strange noises all of the time."
"He's too different," another kid screamed out.

Miss Angelica looked sadly at the children and said, "Different does not mean less than. We are all different in our own special way."

"God made us all different ," Miss Angelica continued. "We are all different colors, shapes, and sizes. What fun would it be if everybody was exactly the same?"

"Believe it or not, we are all gifts from God. However children like Reggie are special gifts. He has a freedom that not many people are fortunate enough to have."

Reggie's mom was off in the distance. She walked over so that she could clearly hear what Miss Angelica had to say.

"What kind of freedom?" Sarah asked.

"Well," Miss Angelica asked, "How many of you would have cried or been sad if people treated you like how you treated Reggie? Let me see a show of hands," she said. Every hand was raised; even Reggie's mommy raised her hand.

"Reggie is a special child because children like him are closer to God than anybody else. This is why the teasing doesn't bother him. He smiles no matter what!"

"He is free because he does not worry about the silly things that everybody else worries about. He doesn't care what people say or think. He loves who he is."

"He is special because even after the meanest things have been done or said to him, he is still happy, loving, and kind. . .
He does not care that people do not understand him. It does not matter that nobody wants to be his friend. God created him with a beautiful heart and loves him no matter what. That is what makes him happy."

"Wow," Reggie's mom said. "He is happy! It has been me that has been so sad because I didn't understand why he was so different. I was too busy paying attention to everything that he couldn't do. I didn't see the beauty in those things that he could." Reggie looked at his mom and kissed her on her cheek.

Miss Angelica smiled. "He is a special lad, and you are special too," she said, looking at Reggie's mom. "God only gives his special gifts to special moms and dads that have special hearts. God knew that you had what it takes to love, raise, and teach such a special little boy."

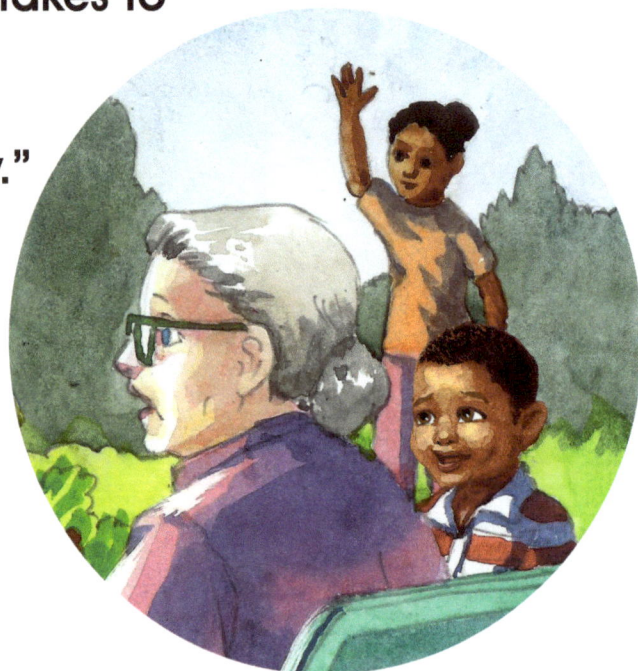

All of the children looked on eagerly waiting for the little old lady to speak again.

"And all of you are special too! It is all of our jobs to respect, protect, and embrace the differences of a person, understanding that although we are all different, nobody is less than or better than anybody else."

"God loves us for who we are and not for who people think we should be. Besides," she winked, "Who is to say what is normal and what is not?"

The children all smiled after listening to what Miss Angelica said. They felt guilty for treating Reggie mean just because he was different. One by one each child apologized to Reggie for teasing him.

The children had a new understanding about Reggie and other kids like him. After hearing Miss Angelica today, they wanted to be different too. They learned it was ok to be yourelf. They also wanted the freedom that comes with being yourself, and not caring what anybody has to say about it. In a sense we all do.

Reggie and his mom walked home happily, hand in hand. All any mother ever wants is for her child to be happy, and for the first time Reggie's mom saw clearly that he had always been. He was happy and favored by God.
He was created exceptionally different.

The End

www.ingramcontent.com/pod-product-compliance
Lightning Source LLC
Chambersburg PA
CBHW041239040426
42445CB00004B/82

* 9 7 8 0 6 9 2 5 4 6 0 0 0 *